CONTENTS

Connect with Latonya Howell
97

THE HEALING DEVOTIONAL

LATONYA HOWELL

THE HEALING DEVOTIONAL

WEEK 1: UNDERSTANDING TRAUMA

Week 1: Hello Trauma: Understanding Trauma

Day 1: Understanding Trauma

Scripture: "The Lord is close to the brokenhearted and saves those who are crushed in spirit." - Psalm 34:18 (NIV)

Passage from the Book: "What is trauma? Simply put, trauma is our emotional response to a terrible event. It has both immediate and long-term reactions. It impacts our emotions, our relationships, and even manifests itself through physical symptoms."

Reflection: Trauma is our emotional response to terrible events, impacting us immediately and long-term. It can paralyze us emotionally and physically, preventing us from moving forward. Trauma affects not only our emotions but also our relationships and physical health. Recognizing and understanding trauma is the first step toward healing. Understanding trauma is crucial for beginning the healing journey. Trauma can stem from various experiences such as abuse, loss, or witnessing a distressing event. The effects of trauma can linger, causing emotional turmoil, physical symptoms like headaches or fatigue, and strained relationships. As a trauma-informed coach, I see firsthand how trauma can halt personal growth and well-being. Acknowledging the impact of trauma validates your experiences and feelings, setting the stage for healing.

Reflection Questions:

- What has been your emotional response to trauma, and how has it affected your life?
- In what ways has trauma influenced your relationships and physical health?

Action Step: Write down your emotions related to a specific trauma. Acknowledge these feelings as a step towards healing.

Day 2: Born into Trauma

Scripture: "Though my father and mother forsake me, the Lord will receive me." - Psalm 27:10 (NIV)

Passage from the Book: "I was born into trauma on Thursday, July 31st, 1986 in Pontiac, Illinois at St. James Hospital. My mother was a drug addict and schizophrenic who ran off to Chicago at the age of eighteen to follow who she thought was the love of her life, only to be forced into prostitution."

Reflection: Most of us are born into trauma, with life circumstances beyond our control setting the tone for our early experiences. Trauma can impact us even before we take our first breath. Prenatal trauma, or trauma that occurs in the womb, happens when a mother experiences stress, illness, substance abuse, or violence during pregnancy. The unborn baby, intimately connected to the mother's emotional and physical state, can absorb these negative experiences. This can lead to long-term effects on the child's emotional and physical health, manifesting in ways such as developmental delays and future emotional and behavioral challenges. The stress hormones that the mother experiences can disrupt the baby's developing brain and stress response systems.

Similarly, preconscious trauma occurs in early childhood, before a child can process or understand traumatic events. Experiences like neglect, abuse, or the sudden loss of a caregiver can deeply impact a child's foundational sense of safety and security. These early traumas can shape emotional and psychological development, potentially leading to attachment issues, anxiety, and emotional regulation difficulties that persist into adulthood. Understanding and addressing these early traumas are crucial steps in our healing journey. By acknowledging the impact of these experiences and seeking healing through faith and supportive interventions, we can work towards restoring our sense of safety and well-being.

Reflection Question:

- Reflect on the circumstances of your birth and early childhood. How have these experiences shaped your view of the world?

Action Step: Spend time in prayer or meditation, asking for healing from any early-life traumas.

Day 3: The Impact of Rejection

Scripture: "When my spirit grows faint within me, it is you who watch over my way." - Psalm 142:3 (NIV)

Passage from the Book: "At an early age, I began dealing with rejection. I felt rejected by my mom. I didn't understand addiction at the time; I just understood that my mom wasn't there."

Reflection: Feelings of rejection, especially from parents, can deeply affect self-worth and emotional stability, leading to long-term impacts. Rejection, particularly from those we look to for love and acceptance, can leave a lasting scar on our hearts. As children, we are especially vulnerable to the actions and absence of our parents. When a parent is emotionally or physically un-available due to addiction, illness, or other circumstances, it often translates to a deep sense of personal rejection. This can severely impact our self-worth, making us feel unworthy of love and af-fection. The absence of a parent's love and approval can lead to a lifelong struggle with feelings of inadequacy and a perpetual fear of being abandoned by others.

This sense of rejection doesn't just affect how we see our-selves; it also shapes our relationships with others. We may be-come overly dependent on the approval of others or, conversely, build emotional walls to prevent further hurt. The long-term im-pacts of rejection can manifest in various ways, including dif-ficulty trusting others, an overwhelming fear of abandonment, and even self-sabotaging behaviors in relationships. It's essential to recognize these patterns and seek healing, knowing that our Heavenly Father watches over us and values us immensely.

Reflection Question:

- How have experiences of rejection influenced your self-worth and relationships?

Action Step: Reach out to a trusted friend, mentor, or coach to discuss your feelings of rejection and seek support.

Day 4: Breaking Generational Curses

Scripture: "I will bless those who bless you and curse those who treat you with contempt. All the families on earth will be blessed through you." - Genesis 12:3 (NLT)

Reflection: Generational trauma and curses can follow families, but awareness and proactive choices can break these cycles.

Passage from the Book: "Some of the trials we deal with in life result from the actions of our ancestors and have little to do with us. In my bloodline, most of the women, for several generations, were never married, had teenage pregnancies, multiple children by different fathers, drug and alcohol addiction, and prostitution."

Reflection Question:

· What generational patterns do you recognize in your family, and how can you break these cycles?

Action Step: Identify one generational pattern you want to break and create a plan to overcome it.

Day 5: The Power of Forgiveness

Scripture: "And you will know the truth, and the truth will set you free." - John 8:32 (NLT)

Reflection: Forgiveness is essential for healing, even when apologies are not given. It frees us from the burden of unresolved pain.

Passage from the Book: "Choosing to forgive, despite not receiving an apology, was one of the first steps towards healing. I might not have been the cause of the trauma, but I was responsible for healing from it."

Reflection Question:

- Is there someone you need to forgive to move forward in your healing journey?

Action Step: Write a letter of forgiveness to someone who has hurt you, even if you don't send it. This can be a powerful step in your healing process.

Day 6: Embracing a Positive Outlook

Scripture: "Rejoice in hope, be patient in tribulation, be constant in prayer." - Romans 12:12 (ESV)

Reflection: Facing trauma with a positive outlook can transform your life. It's about choosing hope and resilience.

Passage from the Book: "When you experience trauma, you will often find yourself at a crossroads. That crossroad has to do with your outlook, and yes, it's your choice."

Reflection Question:

- How can adopting a positive outlook change your approach to dealing with trauma?

Action Step: Start a gratitude journal. Practice gratitude by writing down three things you are thankful for each day, focusing on positive aspects of your life.

Day 7: The Journey to Healing

Scripture: "He heals the brokenhearted and binds up their wounds." - Psalm 147:3 (NIV)

Reflection: Healing from trauma is a journey that requires patience, self-compassion, and support from others.

Passage from the Book: "Regardless of how our trauma comes about, at some point the responsibility of healing from that trauma becomes our own. You may never get the apology you deserve."

Reflection Question:

- What steps can you take today to move forward in your healing journey?

Action Step: Consider seeking guidance from a coach, therapist, or joining a support group to help you navigate your healing process.

WEEK 2: EMBRACING THE JOURNEY OF HEALING

Week 2: Missing Childhood: Embracing the Journey of Healing

Day 1: The Pain of Separation

Scripture: "The Lord is close to the brokenhearted and saves those who are crushed in spirit." - Psalm 34:18 (NIV)

Passage from the Book: "After Ms. Sally picked me up from my mother's house, she took me to a foster home with a woman named Mrs. Houston. I specifically remember driving around the corner from where my mom lived and being dropped off. When I got older and started going to school, I walked past the apartment every day where I had last lived with my mother. I literally relived the trauma of being taken away from my mother almost every day."

Reflection: Separation from loved ones, especially as a child, can create deep emotional scars. These experiences often lead to feelings of abandonment and loss. The pain of being separated from a primary caregiver can linger throughout one's life, impacting relationships and emotional well-being. Understanding and acknowledging this pain is a crucial step towards healing.

Reflection Question:

- What are some experiences in your life that have caused you to feel separated or abandoned? How have these experiences affected you?

Action Step: Write a letter to your younger self, offering comfort and reassurance during those times of separation.

Day 2: Coping with Bullying

Scripture: "But I tell you, love your enemies and pray for those who persecute you." - Matthew 5:44 (NIV)

Passage from the Book: "Robin would do things intentionally to get me in trouble, things like eating foods we weren't supposed to and then blame it on me, or break something and then blame it on me. While I would be getting in trouble for her actions, she would look at me and smirk."

Reflection: Bullying can deeply impact a child's self-esteem and sense of safety. Understanding and addressing these wounds is crucial for healing. The emotional scars from bullying can persist into adulthood, affecting one's self-worth and interpersonal relationships. It's important to confront these experiences and seek healing.

Reflection Question:

- How have you dealt with bullying or unfair treatment in your life? What steps can you take to heal from these experiences?

Action Step: Reach out to a support group or a trusted friend to share your experiences with bullying and seek their support.

Day 3: Physical Trauma and Healing

Scripture: "He heals the brokenhearted and binds up their wounds." - Psalm 147:3 (NIV)

Passage from the Book: "I had third degree burns on my left leg and second degree burns on my right leg and ended up being in the hospital for quite some time. I still have the scars on both of my thighs to this day."

Reflection: Physical trauma leaves visible scars, but the emotional wounds can be just as significant. Healing requires acknowledging both types of pain. Physical trauma can serve as a constant reminder of past pain, making emotional healing even more challenging. Recognizing and addressing both the physical and emotional aspects of trauma is essential for comprehensive healing.

Reflection Question:

- What physical or emotional scars do you carry, and how do they remind you of your past experiences?

Action Step: Spend time in prayer or meditation, asking for healing and strength to accept your scars as part of your journey.

Day 4: The Impact of Abuse

Scripture: "The Lord is a refuge for the oppressed, a stronghold in times of trouble." - Psalm 9:9 (NIV)

Passage from the Book: "I don't know when between him walking me to and from school, and babysitting me that the sexual abuse started, but I know that I began to fear being around him."

Reflection: Abuse, especially during childhood, can profoundly affect one's sense of safety and trust. Overcoming this trauma is a critical part of the healing journey. The impact of abuse can create long-lasting challenges in trusting others and feeling secure. Healing from abuse involves acknowledging the trauma, seeking support, and rebuilding trust in oneself and others.

Reflection Question:

- How has abuse or trauma impacted your ability to trust others? What steps can you take to rebuild trust?

Action Step: Consider seeking professional help or joining a support group to address the impact of abuse and begin the healing process.

Day 5: Dealing with Betrayal

Scripture: "Even if my father and mother abandon me, the Lord will hold me close." - Psalm 27:10 (NLT)

Passage from the Book: "The man with the white beard informed me that Mrs. Houston had reported to the state that I had both started the fire and placed the bag in the baby's crib. I was shocked and heartbroken."

Reflection: Betrayal by those we trust can be deeply wounding. Finding ways to heal from betrayal is essential for moving forward. Betrayal can shake the foundation of our trust and leave us feeling isolated and vulnerable. Healing from betrayal involves processing the hurt, understanding the impact it has had, and finding ways to rebuild trust and move forward.

Reflection Question:

- Have you experienced betrayal by someone you trusted? How can you begin to heal from that betrayal?

Action Step: Write a letter expressing your feelings about the betrayal. You may choose to share it with the person or keep it for your own healing.

Day 6: Finding Hope in Dark Times

Scripture: "I will bless those who bless you and curse those who treat you with contempt. All the families on earth will be blessed through you." - Genesis 12:3 (NLT)

Passage from the Book: "She reached over and placed her hand on my knee, and she said to me, 'I know what you've been through, and I know you didn't do this. Everything will be okay now. I believe you.'"

Reflection: Even in the darkest times, there is hope. Finding moments of light can provide the strength to keep moving forward. In the midst of pain and suffering, it's essential to hold onto hope. These glimmers of light can be the difference between despair and resilience, helping us to navigate through the toughest times.

Reflection Question:

- What moments of hope have you experienced during dark times? How did they help you move forward?

Action Step: Create a gratitude journal to document moments of hope and light in your life. Reflect on these entries regularly.

Day 7: Embracing Healing

Scripture: "And you will know the truth, and the truth will set you free." - John 8:32 (NLT)

Passage from the Book: "For the first time in my life, I envisioned a positive future for myself. To this day, I don't think that Mrs. Bernice knows the impact that she made on my young eleven-year-old life. God is with us, even in the darkest of moments."

Reflection: Healing is a journey that requires time, support, and self-compassion. Embracing the truth of your experiences is a powerful step towards freedom. Healing is not a linear process; it involves ups and downs, patience, and a willingness to confront and accept the truth of our past. By embracing this journey, we can find freedom and peace.

Reflection Question:

- What steps can you take today to embrace your healing journey and envision a positive future?

Action Step: Reach out to a life coach or counselor to discuss your healing journey and set goals for your future. Visit Coach-HERLife.com for additional support and resources.

WEEK 3: SEEKING BELONGING AND OVERCOMING BETRAYAL

Week 3: Family Matters: Seeking Belonging and Overcoming Betrayal

Day 1: The Desire for Family

Scripture: "God sets the lonely in families, he leads out the prisoners with singing." - Psalm 68:6 (NIV)

Passage from the Book: "I desired a family more than anything else in life. I remember watching other kids my age with their families and daydreaming what it would be like to have a home with a mom and a dad."

Reflection: The longing for family and belonging is a deep, intrinsic desire. This chapter explores the impact of not having a stable family and how it shapes one's identity. The absence of a stable family can create a sense of longing and impact one's sense of self and belonging. Recognizing this desire is the first step towards understanding its influence on our lives.

Reflection Question:

- What does family mean to you? How has your experience with family influenced your life?

Action Step: Spend time reflecting on your family experiences and write down how they have shaped your views on family and relationships.

Day 2: Coping with Betrayal

Scripture: "Even my close friend, someone I trusted, one who shared my bread, has turned against me." - Psalm 41:9 (NIV)

Passage from the Book: "One day, we were waiting for the school bus. Ida and I were chatting away as usual. She seemed normal, and I had no indication that anything was wrong. The bus arrived and she asked me to sit in the back of the bus with her. A few minutes later Ida looked at me and then swung at my face."

Reflection: Betrayal by those we trust can be deeply wounding. Understanding and processing these betrayals is essential for healing. Betrayal can leave deep emotional scars and impact our ability to trust others. Healing involves acknowledging the hurt, processing the pain, and finding ways to move forward with grace and resilience.

Reflection Question:

- How have you dealt with betrayal in your life? What steps can you take to heal from these experiences?

Action Step: Write a letter to yourself expressing forgiveness and understanding for the times you have been betrayed.

Day 3: Finding Comfort in Loneliness

Scripture: "The Lord himself goes before you and will be with you; he will never leave you nor forsake you. Do not be afraid; do not be discouraged." - Deuteronomy 31:8 (NIV)

Passage from the Book: "I experienced God for the first time at Mrs. Johnson's house. I remember sitting in my room and talking out loud, expressing my feelings."

Reflection: Loneliness can be overwhelming, but recognizing God's presence can provide comfort and peace. Feeling alone can be a profound and isolating experience. Finding comfort in God's presence can provide the peace and reassurance needed to navigate through these lonely times.

Reflection Question:

- When have you felt the most alone, and how did you cope with it? How can you invite God's presence into your loneliness?

Action Step: Spend time in prayer or meditation, inviting God's presence into your moments of loneliness.

Day 4: Recognizing Your Anointing

Scripture: "The Spirit of the Lord is on me, because he has anointed me to proclaim good news to the poor." - Luke 4:18 (NIV)

Passage from the Book: "I was marked and visible to others whether I wanted to be or not, and that marking is called an anointing."

Reflection: Realizing and accepting one's anointing can be a powerful step towards healing and purpose. Recognizing your anointing means understanding that God has a specific plan and purpose for your life. Embracing this calling can lead to a deeper sense of purpose and fulfillment.

Reflection Question:

- What unique gifts or callings do you believe God has placed on your life? How can you embrace and use them for His glory?

Action Step: Write down your gifts and callings, and pray for guidance on how to use them to fulfill your purpose.

Day 5: Overcoming Negative Words

Scripture: "Gracious words are a honeycomb, sweet to the soul and healing to the bones." - Proverbs 16:24 (NIV)

Passage from the Book: "Mrs. Johnson was a sweet lady for the most part, but she had a mean streak. At times, she would become verbally abusive and tell me things like I would never be anything more than what my mother was."

Reflection: Words have power. This chapter addresses the impact of negative words and how to overcome them. Negative words can leave lasting impacts on our self-esteem and mental health. Overcoming these harmful words involves replacing them with God's truth and affirmations of our worth.

Reflection Question:

- What negative words have been spoken over you, and how have they affected you? How can you replace them with God's truth?

Action Step: Replace negative statements with positive affirmations based on Scripture and speak them over yourself daily.

Day 6: The Power of Forgiveness

Scripture: "Bear with each other and forgive one another if any of you has a grievance against someone. Forgive as the Lord forgave you." - Colossians 3:13 (NIV)

Passage from the Book: "I had to make the choice to forgive her anyway. It is a hard task to forgive someone for hurting you so badly, especially when they have no remorse."

Reflection: Forgiveness is essential for healing. It frees us from the burden of bitterness and allows us to move forward. Forgiveness is not about condoning the actions of others but about freeing ourselves from the hold of resentment and anger. It's a powerful step towards healing and peace.

Reflection Question:

- Who do you need to forgive in your life, and how can you take steps towards forgiving them?

Action Step: Write a letter of forgiveness to someone who has hurt you, even if you don't send it. Release the burden to God.

Day 7: Finding Strength in God

Scripture: "The Lord is my strength and my shield; my heart trusts in him, and he helps me." - Psalm 28:7 (NIV)

Passage from the Book: "I knew that my own personal strength could not get me through this, and I knew that Donald's strength in that moment couldn't get me through. I knew that the only person who could get me through this was the Lord."

Reflection: Relying on God's strength is crucial in overcoming life's challenges and finding peace. Life's challenges can be overwhelming, but finding strength in God provides the resilience and peace needed to navigate through difficult times. Trusting in His strength allows us to face trials with courage and hope.

Reflection Question:

· How have you relied on God's strength in difficult times? How can you continue to trust Him in your current challenges?

Action Step: Spend time in prayer, asking God for strength and guidance in your current situations. Reflect on past times when He has been your strength.

| 31 |

WEEK 4: NAVIGATING JOY AND HEARTACHE

Week 4: The Perfect Life: Navigating Joy and Heartache

Day 1: Adjusting to New Environments

Scripture: "The Lord will guide you always; he will satisfy your needs in a sun-scorched land and will strengthen your frame." - Isaiah 58:11 (NIV)

Passage from the Book: "The first thing I noticed upon my arrival to Utah were the mountains. I arrived in the summer, so they were green and surrounded by clouds. They were so beautiful, but they intimidated me immediately."

Reflection: Adjusting to new environments can be challenging and overwhelming, but God's guidance provides comfort and direction. Moving to a new place or starting a new phase in life can bring about feelings of uncertainty and anxiety. However, remembering that God is always with us, guiding and strengthening us, can help ease these transitions. Embracing new environments with faith allows us to see them as opportunities for growth and new experiences. Trusting in God's plan and leaning on His guidance ensures that we are never alone, no matter how unfamiliar our surroundings may be.

Reflection Question:

- What new environments have you had to adjust to, and how did you cope?
- How can you trust God in new situations?

Action Step: Reflect on a recent change or new environment in your life and write down how you can seek God's guidance in that situation.

Day 2: Building New Relationships

Scripture: "A friend loves at all times, and a brother is born for a time of adversity." - Proverbs 17:17 (NIV)

Passage from the Book: "Meeting Quinton, my biological brother, for the first time, was awkward. We had similarities in the way we looked, yet we knew very little to nothing about each other."

Reflection: Building new relationships, especially with family, can be complex and rewarding. Establishing meaningful connections with others takes time and effort, particularly when it involves reconnecting with biological family members or making new friends in a different environment. These relationships can offer support, love, and a sense of belonging. Understanding that God places people in our lives for specific reasons can help us be more open and intentional in fostering these bonds. Through patience and genuine effort, we can build strong, supportive relationships that enrich our lives.

Reflection Questions:

- What challenges have you faced in building new relationships?
- How can you foster stronger connections with others?

Action Step: Reach out to someone you wish to build a stronger relationship with and plan a meaningful activity together.

Day 3: Facing Cultural Differences

Scripture: "There is neither Jew nor Gentile, neither slave nor free, nor is there male and female, for you are all one in Christ Jesus." - Galatians 3:28 (NIV)

Passage from the Book: "To say that Utah was an adjustment would be an understatement. Everyone was Caucasian, and in the part of town that the Hadley's lived in, everyone was Mormon."

Reflection: Cultural differences can create challenges but also provide opportunities for growth and understanding. Navigating cultural differences requires sensitivity, open-mindedness, and a willingness to learn. Embracing diversity enriches our lives and broadens our perspectives. It allows us to appreciate the unique ways in which God works through different people and cultures. By fostering an attitude of respect and inclusivity, we can build stronger, more harmonious relationships and communities that reflect God's love for all His children.

Reflection Question:

- How have you navigated cultural differences in your life?
- What have you learned from these experiences?

Action Step: Educate yourself about a culture different from your own and find ways to appreciate and understand it better.

Day 4: Embracing Faith

Scripture: "Trust in the Lord with all your heart and lean not on your own understanding." - Proverbs 3:5 (NIV)

Passage from the Book: "On my first visit there, I found the presence of God that I had longed for. A few months after I started attending that church, I accepted Christ into my life, and I was baptized."

Reflection: Embracing faith can provide clarity, comfort, and direction in life's uncertainties. Faith is the cornerstone of our relationship with God. It involves trusting in His wisdom and timing, even when we cannot see the full picture. Embracing faith means surrendering our fears and doubts to God and believing that He will guide us through every situation. It provides a sense of peace and assurance, knowing that God is in control and has a plan for our lives. Deepening our faith through prayer, Bible study, and worship strengthens our connection with God and helps us navigate life's challenges with confidence.

Reflection Question:

- How has your faith journey evolved over time? What steps can you take to deepen your relationship with God?

Action Step: Spend time in prayer and Bible study, seeking to deepen your understanding and relationship with God.

Day 6: Coping with Loss

Scripture: "The Lord is close to the brokenhearted and saves those who are crushed in spirit." - Psalm 34:18 (NIV)

Passage from the Book: "I walked into the room that had been a place of joy, peace, and happiness just a few hours earlier, and saw my daughter, the child I carried for nine months and one week, my future, the one I had desired laying there lifeless."

Reflection: Loss, especially the loss of a child, is devastating. Coping with this loss requires immense strength and faith. Grieving the loss of a loved one, particularly a child, is an incredibly painful and challenging experience. It requires leaning on God's strength and seeking comfort in His promises. Understanding that God is close to the brokenhearted can provide a sense of solace and hope. Allowing ourselves to grieve, seeking support from others, and finding ways to honor and remember our loved ones can help us navigate the difficult journey of loss. Trusting in God's plan and His ability to heal our broken hearts is essential for finding peace and moving forward.

Reflection Question:

- How have you coped with significant losses in your life? What support systems have helped you through these times?

Action Step: Reach out to a grief support group or counselor to discuss your feelings and find support in your journey.

Day 7: Finding Strength in God

Scripture: "I lift up my eyes to the mountains - where does my help come from? My help comes from the Lord, the Maker of heaven and earth." - Psalm 121:1-2 (NIV)

Passage from the Book: "I knew that my own personal strength could not get me through this, and I knew that Donald's strength in that moment couldn't get me through. I knew that the only person who could get me through this was the Lord."

Reflection: Relying on God's strength in the darkest moments is essential for finding peace and moving forward. In times of deep pain and sorrow, recognizing that our strength comes from God can be incredibly empowering. He is our source of comfort, guidance, and strength. Turning to God in prayer, worship, and meditation helps us tap into His infinite power and find the courage to face our challenges. By relying on God's strength, we can overcome obstacles, find peace amidst turmoil, and move forward with hope and resilience.

Reflection Question:

- How have you relied on God's strength during difficult times? How can you continue to trust Him in your current challenges?

Action Step: Spend time in prayer, asking God for strength and guidance in your current situations. Reflect on past times when He has been your strength.

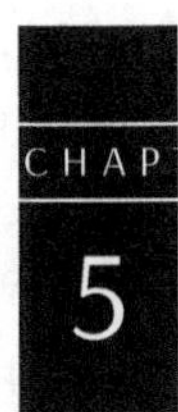

WEEK 5: FINDING FAITH IN THE MIDST OF LOSS

Week 5: God, Is That You?! Finding Faith in the Midst of Loss

Day 1: Embracing God's Peace

Key Scripture: "And the peace of God, which passeth all understanding, shall keep your hearts and minds through Christ Jesus." Philippians 4:7 KJV

Passage from the Book: "Over the next couple of days, I had a roller coaster of emotions. One minute I was crying so hard that I felt as if my heart would stop beating. The next minute I was so calm that you wouldn't know that I was currently living my worst nightmare."

Reflection: Reflect on moments when you experienced God's peace amidst turmoil. God's peace is a profound sense of calm and assurance that transcends our understanding, especially during times of intense emotional pain. This peace is not dependent on our circumstances but is a gift from God that guards our hearts and minds. Embracing God's peace involves trusting in His presence and promises, allowing Him to soothe our anxieties and fears. By focusing on God's unwavering love and faithfulness, we can find solace and strength even in the most challenging times.

Reflection Questions:

- When have you felt God's peace in difficult times?
- How did that peace change your perspective?

Action Step: Write down three things you are grateful for today, acknowledging God's presence in your life.

Day 2: Walking Through the Valley

Key Scripture: "Yea though I walk through the valley of the shadow of death, I will fear no evil: for thou art with me; thy rod and thy staff they comfort me." Psalms 23:4 KJV

Passage from the Book: "I was all the way in the valley of the shadow of death, but I knew that I wasn't alone. I could feel God with me every step of the way."

Reflection: Consider how God has been with you during your darkest moments. Walking through the valleys of life can be daunting, but knowing that God is with us provides comfort and courage. His presence guides and protects us, even when we face the shadow of death or deep despair. Trusting in God's constant companionship helps us navigate these dark times with hope and resilience. Embracing His comfort and guidance allows us to face our fears and find strength in His unwavering support.

Reflection Questions:

- What valleys have you walked through in your life?
- How has God comforted you during these times?

Action Step: Spend five minutes in silent prayer, inviting God's comforting presence into your heart.

Day 3: Strength in Weakness

Key Scripture: "Each time he said, "My grace is all you need. My power works best in weakness." So now I am glad to boast about my weaknesses, so that the power of Christ can work through me." 2 Corinthians 12:9 NLT

Passage from the Book: "I couldn't keep going because I was strong and had it all figured out; in fact, it was quite the opposite. I was able to keep going because I realized that I was completely broken and that only one Person could help me through this tragedy."

Reflection: Identify areas of weakness and see how God's grace has been sufficient for you. Acknowledging our weaknesses allows us to experience God's grace and power more profoundly. In our moments of vulnerability, God's strength is made perfect. By embracing our weaknesses and relying on God's grace, we can find strength and resilience. His grace empowers us to overcome challenges and fulfill His purposes. Understanding that our weaknesses are opportunities for God's power to be displayed helps us trust Him more deeply and live with greater faith and confidence.

Reflection Questions:

- How have you seen God's strength in your weaknesses?
- What does it mean to you to rely on God's grace?

Action Step: Journal about a recent challenge and how you saw God's grace at work in your life.

Day 4: The Decision to Trust

Key Scripture: "I lift up my eyes to the mountains - where does my help come from? My help comes from the Lord, the Maker of heaven and earth." Psalm 121:1-2 NIV

Passage from the Book: "I knew at this point that trusting God was the right thing to do, but that didn't make it any easier."

Reflection: Reflect on the moments when you chose to trust God despite your circumstances. Trusting God is a deliberate choice, especially when faced with uncertainty or adversity. This trust is rooted in the belief that God is sovereign and that His plans are for our good. Choosing to trust God means surrendering our fears, doubts, and need for control to His capable hands. It involves believing that He will provide, guide, and protect us. By making the decision to trust God, we open ourselves to experiencing His peace, guidance, and blessings.

Reflection Questions:

- What are some difficult decisions you've had to trust God with?
- How did choosing to trust Him change the outcome?

Action Step: Write a prayer of trust, surrendering your current struggles to God.

Day 5: Guarding Your Mind and Heart

Key Scripture: "Above all else, guard your heart, for everything you do flows from it." Proverbs 4:23 NIV

Passage from the Book: "I had to guard my mind and protect my heart during this time. When negative thoughts would creep in, I had to find the strength to block them."

Reflection: Understand the importance of protecting your mind and heart from negativity. Guarding our hearts and minds is crucial for maintaining spiritual, emotional, and mental well-being. Negative thoughts and influences can hinder our growth and damage our relationship with God. By being vigilant and intentional about what we allow into our minds and hearts, we can protect ourselves from harmful influences. Filling our minds with God's truth and surrounding ourselves with positive, uplifting influences helps us stay focused on His purposes and maintain a healthy, vibrant faith.

Reflection Questions:

- What steps can you take to guard your heart and mind?
- How do you handle negative thoughts?

Action Step: Create a list of affirmations based on God's promises to combat negative thoughts.

Day 6: Moving Beyond Surface-Level Faith

Key Scripture: "But grow in the grace and knowledge of our Lord and Savior Jesus Christ. To him be glory both now and forever! Amen." 2 Peter 3:18 NIV

Passage from the Book: "There is more to knowing God than just attending church, praying, and listening to worship songs -you know, the Christian basics."

Reflection: Consider how you can deepen your relationship with God beyond the basics. Moving beyond surface-level faith involves a deeper commitment to knowing and following God. It requires intentional effort to grow in our understanding of His Word, character, and will for our lives. This deepening relationship is cultivated through prayer, Bible study, worship, and obedience. As we seek to know God more intimately, we experience His presence and power in new and profound ways. This journey of faith leads to greater spiritual maturity and a more meaningful, impactful life.

Reflection Questions:

- How can you move beyond a surface-level relationship with God?
- What steps can you take to deepen your faith?

Action Step: Commit to a new spiritual practice this week to grow closer to God.

Day 7: Recognizing Distractions

Key Scripture: "Let us throw off everything that hinders and the sin that so easily entangles. And let us run with perseverance the race marked out for us." Hebrews 12:1 NIV

Passage from the Book: "Satan knew it too, and true to his fashion, he set out to distract me and throw me off the path."

Reflection: Identify and remove distractions that hinder your walk with God. Distractions can divert our attention and energy away from God's purposes for our lives. Recognizing these distractions and taking steps to eliminate or minimize them is essential for maintaining focus and fulfilling our God-given calling. This may involve setting boundaries, prioritizing our time, and being intentional about our activities and relationships. By removing distractions, we create space for God to work in and through us, allowing us to run the race He has set before us with perseverance and purpose.

Reflection Questions:

- What distractions are currently hindering your relationship with God?
- How can you remove or minimize these distractions?

Action Step: Make a list of distractions and create a plan to address and remove them from your daily life.

| 51 |

WEEK 6: SELF-AWARENESS AND HEALING

Week 6: Sitting in My Own Mess: Self-Awareness and Healing

Day 1: Recognizing Idolatry

Key Scripture: "See how very much our Father loves us, for he calls us his children, and that is what we are! But the people who belong to this world don't recognize that we are God's children because they don't know him." 1 John 3:1 NLT

Passage from the Book: "I realized that I had created an idol out of marriage. I was at a place in my life where I desired to be married more than I desired a relationship with God."

Reflection: Reflect on areas in your life where you may have created idols. Idolatry occurs when we place anything above our relationship with God. This can include relationships, career, possessions, or even personal desires. Recognizing these idols requires honest self-reflection and a willingness to realign our priorities with God's will. By identifying and letting go of these idols, we can deepen our relationship with God and experience greater freedom and fulfillment in Him.

Reflection Questions:

- What are some things you might be placing above your relationship with God?
- How can you refocus on God as your priority?

Action Step: Write down one idol you need to let go of and pray for God's help to do so.

Day 2: Embracing Self-Awareness

Key Scripture: "For you formed my inward parts; you knitted me together in my mother's womb. I praise you, for I am fearfully and wonderfully made. Wonderful are your works; my soul knows it very well." Psalm 139:13-14 ESV

Passage from the Book: "Self-awareness is being aware of our traits that make us who we are. This includes our positive and negative traits."

Reflection: Consider the importance of self-awareness in your spiritual journey. Self-awareness involves understanding our strengths, weaknesses, and the unique aspects of our personality. This awareness allows us to grow and develop in our relationship with God and others. By embracing self-awareness, we can identify areas for improvement and seek God's guidance in transforming our lives. It also helps us appreciate the unique way God has created us, fostering a deeper sense of self-acceptance and gratitude.

Reflection Questions:

- What positive and negative traits have you discovered about yourself?
- How can you use this self-awareness to grow closer to God?

Action Step: List three traits you are aware of in yourself and how they impact your relationship with God.

Day 3: God's View of You

Key Scripture: "But you are a chosen race, a royal priesthood, a holy nation, a people for his own possession, that you may proclaim the excellencies of him who called you out of darkness into his marvelous light." 1 Peter 2:9 ESV

Passage from the Book: "I began to search and ask myself, 'So, what does God have to say about me?'"

Reflection: Meditate on what God says about you. Understanding how God views us is essential for building a healthy self-image and fulfilling our purpose. The Bible is filled with affirmations of our identity in Christ, reminding us that we are loved, chosen, and valuable. Meditating on these truths helps us combat negative self-perceptions and align our thoughts with God's perspective. This shift in mindset empowers us to live confidently and purposefully, knowing that we are deeply loved and valued by our Creator.

Reflection Questions:

- How do you see yourself compared to how God sees you?
- What scriptures can you use to remind yourself of your identity in Christ?

Action Step: Write down and memorize three Bible verses that affirm your identity in God.

Day 4: Preparing for Wholeness

Key Scripture: "But it was to us that God revealed these things by his Spirit. For his Spirit searches out everything and shows us God's deep secrets." 1 Corinthians 2:10 NLT

Passage from the Book: "Growing closer to God, combined with getting to know the real me and sitting in my own mess, revealed to me how broken I truly was and started me on a path of healing and wholeness."

Reflection: Reflect on how self-awareness and God's revelations lead to wholeness. Wholeness involves recognizing our brokenness and seeking God's healing and restoration. By becoming self-aware and allowing God to reveal areas that need healing, we can embark on a journey towards wholeness. This process requires humility, honesty, and a willingness to surrender our pain and struggles to God. Through His Spirit, God guides us towards healing, helping us become whole and healthy individuals who reflect His love and grace.

Reflection Questions:

- What areas of brokenness has God revealed to you?
- How has this revelation helped you in your healing process?

Action Step: Spend time in prayer, asking God to reveal areas that need healing and wholeness in your life.

Day 5: Accountability and Apology

Key Scripture: "But when he, the Spirit of truth, comes, he will guide you into all the truth. He will not speak on his own; he will speak only what he hears, and he will tell you what is yet to come." John 16: 13 NIV

Passage from the Book: "I knew that for full healing to take place, I needed to apologize to my ex-husband for the role that I played."

Reflection: Understand the importance of accountability in your spiritual growth. Accountability involves taking responsibility for our actions and seeking to make amends where necessary. Apologizing for our mistakes and seeking forgiveness is a crucial part of this process. It allows us to repair relationships and grow in humility and integrity. By being accountable to others and to God, we can experience deeper healing and transformation in our lives.

Reflection Questions:

- Who do you need to seek accountability with in your life?
- How can apologizing and taking responsibility lead to healing?

Action Step: Reach out to someone you need to apologize to and seek to make amends.

Day 6: Intentional Serving

Key Scripture: "Therefore go and make disciples of all nations, baptizing them in the name of the Father and of the Son and of the Holy Spirit," Matthew 28:19 NIV

Passage from the Book: "I was busy in the church, but I was busy doing absolutely nothing."

Reflection: Reflect on how you can serve God more intentionally. Serving with intention means aligning our actions with God's purposes and seeking to make a meaningful impact. This requires evaluating our current commitments and ensuring that our service is fruitful and aligned with God's will. By serving intentionally, we can make a positive difference in the lives of others and grow in our relationship with God. It involves being purposeful and prayerful in our actions, seeking to honor God in all that we do.

Reflection Questions:

- Are you serving with intention or out of obligation?
- How can you better align your service with God's purpose for you?

Action Step: Evaluate your current commitments and make necessary adjustments to serve more effectively.

Day 7: Trusting God with Your Path

Key Scripture: "Trust in the Lord with all your heart and lean not on your own understanding; in all your ways submit to him, and he will make your paths straight." Proverbs 3:5-6 NIV

Passage from the Book: "My daily prayer was 'God, please place me where You would have me to be and allow me to do what is pleasing to you.' Things in my life started changing, and not all the changes felt like they were for my good."

Reflection: Consider how trusting God can reshape your path. Trusting God involves surrendering our plans and desires to His will. It requires faith that He knows what is best for us and will guide us on the right path. This trust is not always easy, especially when His plans differ from our expectations. However, by submitting to God's guidance and trusting in His wisdom, we can experience greater peace and fulfillment. Trusting God with our path allows us to live with purpose and confidence, knowing that He is leading us towards His perfect plan.

Reflection Questions:

- What areas of your life do you need to trust God with more?
- How can submitting to God's will change your life?

Action Step: Pray and ask God to guide your steps and show you His purpose for your life.

WEEK 7: TRUSTING GOD IN UNCERTAINTY

Week 7: The Wilderness Period: Trusting God in Uncertainty

Day 1: Letting Go

Key Scripture: "My old self has been crucified with Christ. It is no longer I who live, but Christ lives in me. So I live in this earthly body by trusting in the Son of God, who loved me and gave himself for me." Galatians 2:20 NLT

Passage from the Book: "The journey requires us to let people go from time to time. The challenge is in trusting the process and learning to be okay with letting certain people go."

Reflection: Reflect on the importance of letting go of relationships that are no longer aligned with your spiritual journey. Letting go can be one of the most challenging aspects of spiritual growth, especially when it involves people we care deeply about. However, there are times when maintaining certain relationships can hinder our progress and keep us from fulfilling God's purpose in our lives. Trusting in God's plan often requires releasing those who are not meant to walk with us on our path. This act of letting go is not just about ending relationships but about making room for new, divine connections that will support and uplift us.

Reflection Questions:

- Who do you need to let go of in your life to grow spiritually?
- How can letting go be an act of trusting God?

Action Step: Write down one relationship you need to release and pray for strength to let it go.

Day 2: Embracing Change

Key Scripture: "And he said to all, "If anyone would come after me, let him deny himself and take up his cross daily and follow me. For whoever would save his life will lose it, but whoever loses his life for my sake will save it." Luke 9:23-24 ESV

Passage from the Book: "I had people question my judgment, my character, and my relationship with God. That's the thing though, I wasn't looking for it to make sense to others; I was looking for it to make sense to me and to align with what God was directing me to do."

Reflection: consider how change can be a necessary part of spiritual growth. Embracing change is essential for personal and spiritual development. Change can be daunting, often bringing uncertainty and discomfort. Yet, it is through these changes that God shapes and molds us into the people He wants us to be. Embracing change means trusting that God's plans are for our good, even when we do not understand them. It involves stepping out in faith, knowing that every change is a step towards a greater purpose and closer relationship with God.

Reflection Questions:

- How do you handle change that others don't understand?
- What changes has God called you to make that require faith?

Action Step: List three changes you feel God is directing you to make and pray for courage to follow through.

Day 3: Finding Your Church Home

Key Scripture: "Therefore go and make disciples of all nations, baptizing them in the name of the Father and of the Son and of the Holy Spirit," Matthew 28:19 NIV

Passage from the Book: "I began to search for a church that was more in alignment with where I knew that God was directing me."

Reflection: Reflect on the importance of finding a spiritual community that aligns with your calling. Finding the right church home is crucial for spiritual growth and fulfillment. A church should not just be a place you attend but a community where you feel spiritually nourished and supported. It should align with your beliefs and help you grow in your faith. This search can be challenging but finding a church that feels like home will provide a solid foundation for your spiritual journey. It's about finding a community that encourages you to live out your faith authentically and helps you fulfill your God-given purpose.

Reflection Questions:

- What qualities do you look for in a church community?
- How can a church help you fulfill your spiritual calling?

Action Step: Research and visit one new church that aligns with your spiritual goals, or create a list of qualities that you appreciate in your current church.

Day 4: Obedience to God

Key Scripture: "Yea though I walk through the valley of the shadow of death, I will fear no evil: for thou art with me; thy rod and thy staff they comfort me." Psalms 23:4 KJV

Passage from the Book: "Being obedient to God often doesn't make sense because it's not meant to make sense."

Reflection: Understand the importance of obedience to God's direction, even when it doesn't make sense. Obedience to God is fundamental in our walk of faith, especially when His instructions don't align with our understanding or desires. It requires a deep trust in His wisdom and timing. Obeying God means stepping out of our comfort zones and surrendering our plans for His. This act of faith can lead to profound personal growth and divine blessings. It is in these moments of obedience that we truly experience God's presence and guidance, even when the path ahead seems unclear.

Reflection Questions:

- When have you felt called to be obedient to God despite not understanding?
- How did your obedience impact your spiritual journey?

Action Step: Identify one area where you need to be more obedient to God and commit to it.

Day 5: Divine Support

Key Scripture: "My old self has been crucified with Christ. It is no longer I who live, but Christ lives in me. So I live in this earthly body by trusting in the Son of God, who loved me and gave himself for me." Galatians 2:20 NLT

Passage from the Book: "God sends exactly who we need when we need them. Angels truly do walk among us, and God assigns them to us."

Reflection: Reflect on how God places people in your life to support you. Divine support often comes through the people God places in our lives. These individuals can provide the encouragement, wisdom, and love we need to navigate challenging seasons. Recognizing and appreciating these divine connections is crucial, as they are often answers to our prayers for support and guidance. These relationships are not coincidental but are orchestrated by God to help us fulfill His purpose for our lives. Being open to receiving support from others is a sign of humility and trust in God's provision.

Reflection Questions:

- Who has God placed in your life to support your spiritual journey?
- How can you show gratitude for their support?

Action Step: Write a thank-you note to someone who has been a spiritual support to you, and give it to them.

Day 6: Trusting God's Plan

Key Scripture: "And we know that in all things God works for the good of those who love him, who have been called according to his purpose." Romans 8:28 NIV

Passage from the Book: "Here I was still in the middle of my 'wilderness period,' feeling so alone, and God had taken away from me the one person who truly understood me and encouraged me."

Reflection: Trust in God's plan, even when it involves loss or hardship. Trusting in God's plan means believing that He is working all things for our good, even when we face loss or hardship. It involves surrendering our understanding and embracing His higher purpose. This trust can be challenging, especially when the path is painful and unclear. However, holding on to the promise that God is in control and has a purpose for everything we endure can provide comfort and strength. It is about believing that His plans are for our ultimate good and His glory.

Reflection Questions:

- How have you seen God work through difficult times in your life?
- What have you learned about God's faithfulness during these times?

Action Step: Write a prayer, expressing your trust in God's plan, even through hardships.

Day 7: Walking in Purpose

Key Scripture: "For I know the plans I have for you," declares the Lord, "plans to prosper you and not to harm you, plans to give you hope and a future." Jeremiah 29:11 NIV

Passage from the Book: "My life has never been my own; each life experience that I encountered has served a purpose, and that purpose was to bring glory to God's name."

Reflection: Reflect on how God's purpose unfolds through your journey. Walking in purpose means aligning your life with God's plans and intentions for you. It involves seeking His guidance and being willing to step out in faith, even when the way forward is not entirely clear. Understanding that every experience, including the trials and challenges, is part of God's plan to shape you and prepare you for His purpose can bring a sense of peace and direction. Embracing your purpose requires continual prayer, trust, and obedience to God's leading.

Reflection Questions:

- How have your life experiences shaped your spiritual purpose?
- What steps can you take to walk more fully in God's purpose for you?

Action Step: Set one goal for the next month that aligns with God's purpose for your life and take the first step towards it.

WEEK 8: NAVIGATING GRIEF AND HEALING

Week 8: The Healing Begins - Or Does It?: Navigating Grief and Healing

Day 1: Understanding Healing

Key Scripture: "For I know the plans I have for you, declares the Lord, plans to prosper you and not to harm you, plans to give you hope and a future." Jeremiah 29:11 NIV

Passage from the Book: "Healing is not the absence of the pain; it's learning how to manage that pain."

Reflection: Reflect on how healing is a journey, not a destination. Healing from trauma and grief is a complex and ongoing process. It involves addressing and managing pain rather than eliminating it. Understanding that healing is a journey allows us to be patient and compassionate with ourselves. It requires a commitment to continuous growth and self-care. By viewing healing as a journey, we can embrace the ups and downs and recognize that each step forward is progress. This perspective helps us maintain hope and resilience, knowing that God is with us every step of the way.

Reflection Questions:

- What misconceptions do you have about healing?
- How can you shift your focus to managing pain rather than eliminating it?

Action Step: Write down your current understanding of healing and identify areas where you need to adjust your perspective.

Day 2: The Roller Coaster of Grief

Key Scripture: "And the peace of God, which passeth all understanding, shall keep your hearts and minds through Christ Jesus." Philippians 4:7 KJV

Passage from the Book: "I went from being completely content, to having a thought about my daughter that took me right back to the day she died."

Reflection: Consider how grief can come in waves and the importance of allowing yourself to feel. Grief is not a linear process; it often comes in unpredictable waves. Allowing ourselves to feel and process these emotions is essential for healing. Denying or suppressing grief can hinder our progress and prolong our pain. By acknowledging and expressing our feelings, we can begin to heal and find peace. It's important to remember that it's okay to grieve and that God's peace is available to us even in our darkest moments. Embracing our grief with honesty and compassion helps us navigate the roller coaster of emotions with grace and resilience.

Reflection Questions:

- How do you handle unexpected waves of grief?
- What can you do to allow yourself to feel and process these emotions?

Action Step: Identify and implement one healthy coping mechanism for when waves of grief hit.

Day 3: Compassion in Grief

Key Scripture: "Yea though I walk through the valley of the shadow of death, I will fear no evil: for thou art with me; thy rod and thy staff they comfort me." Psalms 23:4 KJV

Passage from the Book: "Learn to be compassionate towards yourself as you journey through grief."

Reflection: Reflect on the importance of self-compassion and compassion towards others in grief. Showing compassion to ourselves and others during grief is crucial for healing. Self-compassion involves being gentle and understanding with ourselves, acknowledging our pain, and allowing ourselves to grieve without judgment. Extending compassion to others who are grieving helps create a supportive environment where healing can occur. It involves listening, offering comfort, and being present for those who are hurting. Compassion fosters connection and provides the emotional support needed to navigate the difficult journey of grief.

Reflection Questions:

- In what ways can you show more compassion to yourself in your grief journey?
- How can you extend compassion to others who are grieving?

Action Step: Write a compassionate letter to yourself acknowledging your grief and pain.

Day 4: The Role of Therapy

Key Scripture: "But it was to us that God revealed these things by his Spirit. For his Spirit searches out everything and shows us God's deep secrets." 1 Corinthians 2:10 NLT

Passage from the Book: "Seeking a therapist is not a reflection of your faith level with God. It reflects your desire to be healed."

Reflection: Understand the importance of seeking therapy and how it complements your faith. Seeking therapy is a valuable and necessary step in the healing process. It provides a safe space to explore and address our pain with the guidance of a trained professional. Therapy, combined with faith, can lead to profound healing and transformation. It is not a reflection of weak faith but a demonstration of our commitment to healing and wholeness. Therapy offers tools and strategies to manage pain, process trauma, and develop healthier coping mechanisms. Embracing both therapy and faith allows us to experience comprehensive healing and growth.

Reflection Questions:

- What are your thoughts on seeking therapy?
- How can therapy and faith work together in your healing journey?

Action Step: Research and reach out to a therapist who aligns with your needs and values.

Day 5: Responsibility in Healing

Key Scripture: "I have told you these things, so that in me you may have peace. In this world you will have trouble. But take heart! I have overcome the world." John 16:33 NIV

Passage from the Book: "You may not have chosen what happened to you, but you absolutely can control how it impacts your life moving forward."

Reflection: Reflect on taking responsibility for your healing and not letting past traumas define your future. Taking responsibility for our healing involves recognizing that while we may not have control over what happened to us, we do have control over our response. It means choosing to seek healing, forgiveness, and growth rather than remaining stuck in pain and resentment. This responsibility empowers us to take proactive steps towards healing and transformation. It involves seeking support, developing healthy coping mechanisms, and trusting God to guide us through the process. By taking ownership of our healing journey, we can move forward with hope and resilience.

Reflection Questions:

- What steps can you take to take responsibility for your healing?
- How can you prevent past traumas from controlling your future?

Action Step: Set a goal to work on one specific area of your life impacted by past trauma.

Day 6: Moving Beyond Blame

Key Scripture: "Each time he said, "My grace is all you need. My power works best in weakness." So now I am glad to boast about my weaknesses, so that the power of Christ can work through me." 2 Corinthians 12:9 NLT

Passage from the Book: "Move away from this mindset. It's damaging and far too often it holds us back and prevents us from reaching our true destiny."

Reflection: Consider how shifting away from blame can accelerate your healing process. Blame can keep us trapped in a cycle of pain and bitterness. Moving beyond blame involves taking responsibility for our healing and letting go of resentment towards those who hurt us. It requires a shift in mindset, recognizing that holding onto blame hinders our growth and healing. By releasing blame, we can focus on our own healing and development. This shift allows us to experience God's grace and power in our lives, transforming our pain into strength and resilience.

Reflection Questions:

- Who or what do you need to stop blaming for your current situation?
- How can taking ownership help you move forward?

Action Step: Identify one area where you've been placing blame and write down steps to take ownership instead.

Day 7: Embracing the Journey

Key Scripture: "In this world you will have trouble. But take heart! I have overcome the world." John 16:33 NIV

Passage from the Book: "Overcoming trauma in one area doesn't make you exempt from trauma in other areas. As long as we are alive, the journey never gets easier."

Reflection: Reflect on the continuous journey of healing and how it shapes your faith. Healing is an ongoing process that requires patience, perseverance, and faith. Embracing the journey involves recognizing that healing takes time and that setbacks are a natural part of the process. It requires trusting God to guide us and provide the strength we need to keep moving forward. By embracing the journey, we can develop a deeper faith and reliance on God. This perspective helps us navigate the challenges of healing with hope and resilience, knowing that God is with us every step of the way.

Reflection Questions:

- How has your healing journey shaped your faith?
- What can you do to stay committed to your healing process?

Action Step: Commit to a daily practice that supports your ongoing healing journey, such as journaling or prayer.

WEEK 9: EMBRACING A PURPOSEFUL LIFE

Week 9: Intentional Living: Embracing a Purposeful Life

Day 1: Defining Intentional Living

Key Scripture: "May the favor of the Lord our God rest on us; establish the work of our hands for us - yes, establish the work of our hands." Psalms 90:17 (NIV)

Passage from the Book: "To live intentionally means to go through the process of healing by stretching and/or extending yourself."

Reflection: Consider what it means to live intentionally and how it aligns with God's purpose for your life. Intentional living involves making deliberate choices that align with God's purposes for our lives. It means being mindful of our actions, decisions, and priorities, ensuring that they reflect our faith and values. Living intentionally requires setting goals, making plans, and taking actions that lead us towards fulfilling God's calling. By living with intention, we can experience greater fulfillment and purpose, knowing that our lives are aligned with God's will.

Reflection Questions:

- What does intentional living mean to you?
- How can you begin to incorporate intentionality in your daily life?

Action Step: Write down one area of your life where you want to start living more intentionally and make a plan to do so.

Day 2: Waiting with Purpose

Key Scripture: "Preach the word; be prepared in season and out of season; correct, rebuke and encourage—with great patience and careful instruction." 2nd Timothy 4:2 (NIV)

Passage from the Book: "Sometimes the test is waiting."

Reflection: Reflect on the importance of serving God while waiting for His promises to be fulfilled. Waiting for God's promises can be challenging, but it is an opportunity to grow in faith and service. Serving God while we wait helps us stay focused on His purposes and develop patience and perseverance. It involves being faithful in our daily tasks, seeking to honor God in all that we do. By serving with purpose, we can make the most of our waiting periods, growing spiritually and impacting the lives of others.

Reflection Questions:

- What promise from God are you currently waiting for?
- How can you serve God more intentionally during this waiting period?

Action Step: Identify a way to serve in your community or church while you wait for God's promises.

Day 3: Intentional Service

Key Scripture: "Do everything in love" 1 Corinthians 16:14 (NIV)

Passage from the Book: "Was I serving productively and being fruitful? That's a hard NO!"

Reflection: Reflect on the difference between serving productively and being busy without purpose. Intentional service means serving with a clear purpose and focus, rather than just being busy. It involves evaluating our commitments and ensuring that our service aligns with God's calling and purposes. By serving intentionally, we can make a meaningful impact and avoid burnout. It requires being mindful of our motives and seeking to serve out of love and obedience to God. Intentional service leads to greater fulfillment and effectiveness in our ministry.

Reflection Questions:

- Are there areas in your life where you are busy but not productive?
- How can you shift your focus to serve more intentionally?

Action Step: Evaluate your current commitments and identify one area where you can serve with more intention.

Day 4: Intentional Relationships

Key Scripture: "Whatever you do, work at it with all your heart, as working for the Lord, not for human masters." Colossians 3:23-24 (NIV)

Passage from the Book: "Staying in the relationship and being intentional about where the relationship was going is where I had trouble."

Reflection: Reflect on the importance of being intentional in your relationships, especially in dating and marriage. Building intentional relationships involves being purposeful and thoughtful in how we connect with others. It means asking meaningful questions, setting clear expectations, and seeking to build deep, authentic connections. In dating and marriage, intentionality helps foster trust, communication, and mutual respect. By being intentional in our relationships, we can create strong, healthy bonds that reflect God's love and grace.

Reflection Questions:

- How can you be more intentional in your current relationships?
- What intentional questions can you start asking to build deeper connections?

Action Step: Write down three intentional questions to ask in your relationships to foster deeper connections.

Day 5: Intentional Career Growth

Key Scripture: "And God is able to bless you abundantly, so that in all things at all times, having all that you need, you will abound in every good work." 2 Corinthians 9:8 (NIV)

Passage from the Book: "I became intentional about excelling in my craft. I studied hard and became a certified human resource professional."

Reflection: Reflect on the importance of being intentional in your career and how it aligns with God's purpose for your life. Intentional career growth involves setting clear goals, seeking opportunities for development, and aligning our work with God's purposes. It means being proactive in our career planning, seeking God's guidance, and taking steps to advance our skills and knowledge. By being intentional in our career growth, we can achieve greater success and fulfillment, knowing that our work is aligned with God's will and purpose.

Reflection Questions:

- What are your career goals and how can you be more intentional in achieving them?
- How does your career align with God's purpose for your life?

Action Step: Set one career goal and create a step-by-step plan to achieve it, including prayer and trust in God's provision.

Day 6: Intentional Healing

Key Scripture: "For I know the plans I have for you, declares the Lord, plans to prosper you and not to harm you, plans to give you hope and a future." Jeremiah 29:11 (NIV)

Passage from the Book: "Be intentional about living, be intentional about healing, and be intentional about finding the necessity in your trauma."

Reflection: Reflect on the role of intentionality in your healing journey and how it impacts your overall well-being. Intentional healing involves actively seeking to address and manage our pain and trauma. It requires a commitment to self-care, therapy, and spiritual growth. By being intentional about our healing, we can experience greater wholeness and well-being. This involves setting goals, seeking support, and taking proactive steps to heal. Intentional healing helps us overcome our past and move forward with hope and resilience.

Reflection Questions:

- What steps can you take to be more intentional about your healing process?
- How can intentionality in healing improve your quality of life?

Action Step: Identify one area of your healing journey where you need to be more intentional and take a specific step towards it.

Day 7: Living with Intention

Key Scripture: "Whatever you do, work at it with all your heart, as working for the Lord, not for human masters, since you know that you will receive an inheritance from the Lord as a reward. It is the Lord Christ you are serving." Colossians 3:23-24(NIV)

Passage from the Book: "When you learn to be intentional in your life, things start to happen - not only to you, but for you."

Reflection: Reflect on how living with intention in all areas of your life can lead to a more fulfilled and purpose-driven existence. Living with intention involves making deliberate choices that reflect our faith and values. It means setting clear goals, being mindful of our actions, and seeking to honor God in all that we do. By living intentionally, we can experience greater fulfillment, purpose, and alignment with God's will. It requires a commitment to continuous growth, self-reflection, and seeking God's guidance in all areas of our lives.

Reflection Questions:

- How can you incorporate intentionality into every aspect of your life?
- What changes do you need to make to live more intentionally?

Action Step: Commit to a daily practice of intentional living, such as setting daily intentions or reflecting on your actions at the end of each day.

WEEK 10: TRUSTING IN GOD'S TIMING

Week 10: Trusting in God's Timing

Day 1: Waiting on God

Scripture: "But those who wait on the Lord shall renew their strength; they shall mount up with wings like eagles, they shall run and not be weary, they shall walk and not faint." - Isaiah 40:31 (NKJV)

Passage from the Book: "I've learned that waiting on God is an active process. It's not about sitting idly by but continuing to serve, trust, and seek Him, knowing that His timing is perfect."

Reflection: Waiting on God can be one of the most challenging aspects of our faith journey. It's in these moments of waiting that our trust and patience are truly tested. We may feel anxious or impatient, but waiting on God is never wasted time. It is in these seasons that God renews our strength, preparing us for the journey ahead. Just as an eagle soars effortlessly through the sky, those who wait on the Lord are lifted above their circumstances, finding new strength and perspective.

Reflection Questions:

- What are you currently waiting on God for?

- How can you actively seek Him during this waiting period?

Action Step: Spend time in prayer, asking God for patience and strength as you wait for His timing.

Day 2: Trusting God's Plan

Scripture: "For I know the plans I have for you, declares the Lord, plans to prosper you and not to harm you, plans to give you hope and a future." - Jeremiah 29:11 (NIV)

Passage from the Book: "Through every trial and triumph, I've learned to trust that God's plan is always for my good, even when it doesn't align with my own expectations."

Reflection: Trusting God's plan requires surrendering our own desires and timelines. It means believing that His plans are greater than ours, even when we don't understand them. God's plans are designed to prosper us, to give us hope and a future. This promise assures us that, despite our current circumstances, God's ultimate plan for our lives is good.

Reflection Questions:

- How have you seen God's plan unfold in your life in unexpected ways?

- What areas of your life do you need to surrender to God's plan?

Action Step: Write a prayer of surrender, giving your plans and desires to God and trusting in His greater plan for your life.

Day 3: Embracing Uncertainty

Scripture: "Trust in the Lord with all your heart and lean not on your own understanding; in all your ways submit to him, and he will make your paths straight." - Proverbs 3:5-6 (NIV)

Passage from the Book: "In times of uncertainty, I've found peace in knowing that I don't have to have it all figured out. God's understanding is far greater than mine, and His guidance is always sure."

Reflection: Embracing uncertainty means acknowledging that we don't have all the answers and that's okay. It requires trusting in God's wisdom over our own and submitting to His guidance. When we lean not on our understanding but on God's, He promises to direct our paths, leading us in the way we should go.

Reflection Questions:

- What uncertainties are you facing right now?

- How can you trust God's guidance in these uncertain times?

Action Step: Take a step of faith in an area of uncertainty, trusting that God will guide you.

Day 4: Patience in Trials

Scripture: "Consider it pure joy, my brothers and sisters, whenever you face trials of many kinds, because you know that the testing of your faith produces perseverance." - James 1:2-3 (NIV)

Passage from the Book: "Every trial I've faced has been a stepping stone in my faith journey, teaching me patience and reliance on God's strength."

Reflection: Patience in trials is a virtue that strengthens our faith. Trials are not meant to break us but to build us up, developing perseverance and character. Embracing trials with joy is a testament to our trust in God's refining process. Each trial we face is an opportunity for growth, a chance to become more like Christ.

Reflection Questions:

· How have trials in your life strengthened your faith?

· What can you learn from your current challenges?

Action Step: Identify a current trial and find reasons to be thankful for it, focusing on the growth it can bring.

Day 5: Trusting God's Provision

Scripture: "And my God will meet all your needs according to the riches of his glory in Christ Jesus." - Philippians 4:19 (NIV)

Passage from the Book: "God's provision has been evident in my life, not always in the way I expected, but always in the way I needed."

Reflection: Trusting God's provision means believing that He will supply all our needs. It's about having faith that God, in His infinite resources, knows what we need and will provide at the right time. His provision is not just about material needs but also emotional, spiritual, and relational needs.

Reflection Questions:

- How have you seen God's provision in your life?

- What needs do you need to trust God to provide for?

Action Step: Make a list of your needs and pray, trusting God to meet each one in His perfect timing.

Day 6: Walking in Faith

Scripture: "For we live by faith, not by sight." - 2 Corinthians 5:7 (NIV)

Passage from the Book: "Walking in faith has taught me to rely on God's promises rather than my perception. It's a journey of trust and obedience."

Reflection: Walking in faith means trusting in what we cannot see, believing in God's promises even when circumstances seem contrary. Faith is the assurance of things hoped for, the conviction of things not seen. It's about moving forward with confidence, knowing that God is with us every step of the way.

Reflection Questions:

· What areas of your life require more faith?

· How can you practice walking by faith daily?

Action Step: Take a step of faith in an area where you've been hesitant, trusting God to lead you.

Day 7: Celebrating God's Timing

Scripture: "He has made everything beautiful in its time." - Ecclesiastes 3:11 (NIV)

Passage from the Book: "Looking back, I can see how God's timing has been perfect in my life, even when I didn't understand it at the moment."

Reflection: Celebrating God's timing means recognizing and appreciating that His timing is perfect. It might not align with our schedules, but it is always right. God's timing brings beauty and purpose to our lives. Trusting in His timing allows us to see the bigger picture and celebrate the journey, knowing that He is in control.

Reflection Questions:

- How have you seen God's perfect timing in your life?

- What can you do to celebrate God's timing in your current situation?

Action Step: Reflect on past experiences where God's timing was evident and write a gratitude letter to God, thanking Him for His perfect timing. Reflect on your journey through "The Healing Devotional" by considering your personal growth, emotional breakthroughs, challenges overcome, key insights gained, and the impact on your relationships and daily practices. How have these experiences shaped your mindset, supported your healing, and influenced your future goals?

CONNECT WITH LATONYA HOWELL

Connect with Latonya Howell

Thank you for embarking on this healing journey with me through "The Healing Devotional: Inspired by The Trauma Was Necessary." Your progress and transformation are important to me, and I would love to stay connected and continue supporting your growth. Here are several ways you can reach out and stay in touch:

Website: Visit my website www.coachherlife.com for more resources, blog posts, and information about my coaching services. You can also sign up for my newsletter to receive regular updates and exclusive content.

Social Media: Follow me on Instagram for daily inspiration, updates, and interactive content:

- **Instagram: @coachherlife**

· **Email:** Feel free to reach out via email for any inquiries, coaching questions, or to share your personal journey with me:

· **Email:** latonyalhowell@gmail.com

LinkedIn: Connect with me on LinkedIn to stay updated on my professional journey, new projects, and events:

· **LinkedIn:** https://www.linkedin.com/in/latonyahowell/

Speaking Engagements and Workshops: Interested in having me speak at your event or conduct a workshop? I offer sessions on trauma-informed practices, personal development, career development and more. Reach out to discuss opportunities:

· **Contact:** Speaking Engagements

Book Purchases: You can purchase "The Trauma Was Necessary" and other books through these retailers:

· **Amazon**

- **Barnes & Noble**

- **Target**

- **Walmart**

Share Your Story: I would love to hear about your experiences and how "The Healing Devotional" has impacted your life. Share your story on social media using the hashtag #TheHealingDevotional and tag me for a chance to be featured.

Thank you for being a part of this journey. Together, we can continue to heal, grow, and inspire each other.

With gratitude,

Latonya Howell

www.ingramcontent.com/pod-product-compliance
Lightning Source LLC
Chambersburg PA
CBHW072019150726
47999CB00002B/730